WONDERFUL NATURAL WONDERS

THE ROCKY MOUNTAINS

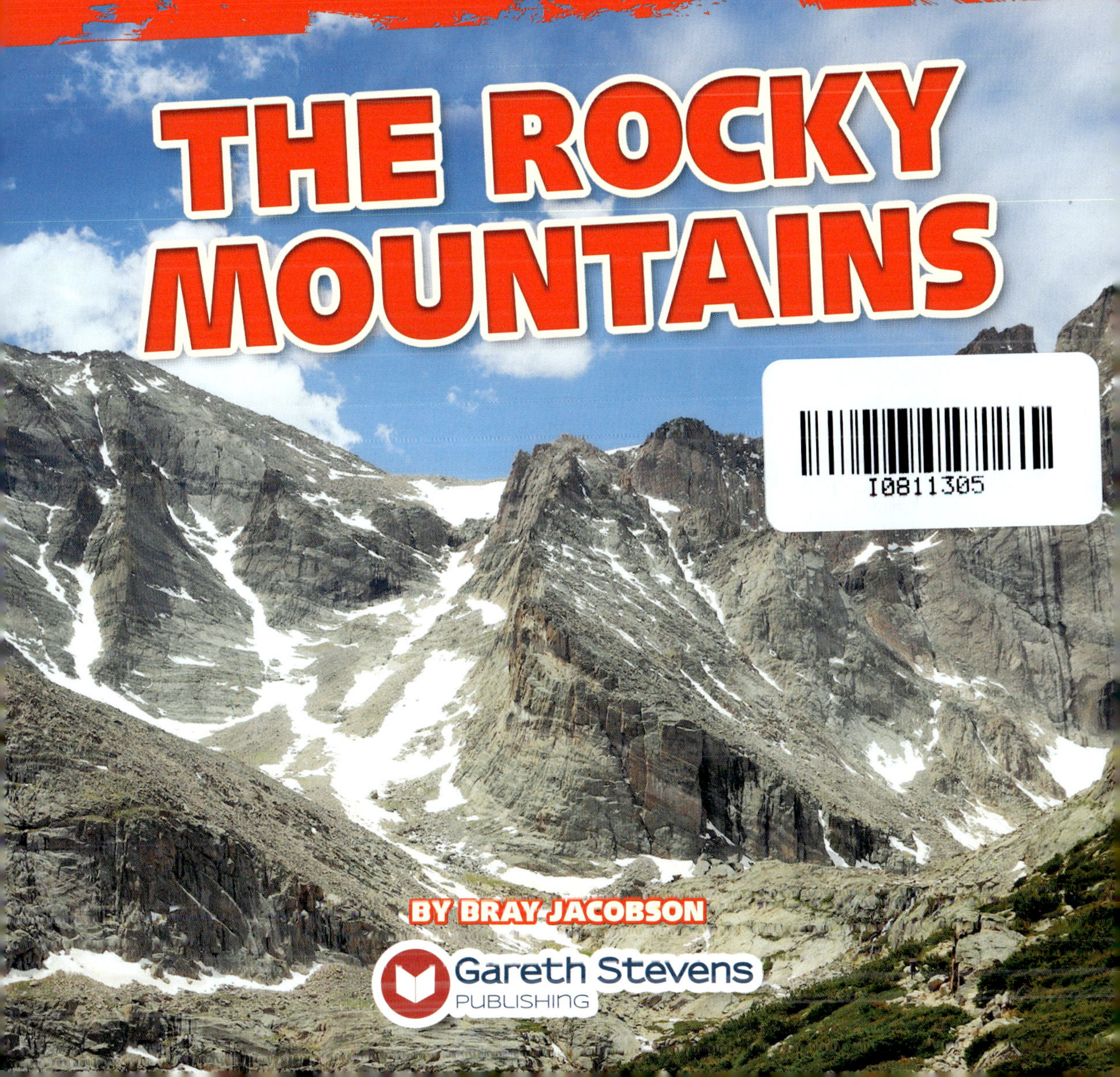

BY BRAY JACOBSON

Gareth Stevens PUBLISHING

Please visit our website, www.garethstevens.com. For a free color catalog of all our high-quality books, call toll free 1-800-542-2595 or fax 1-877-542-2596.

Library of Congress Cataloging-in-Publication Data
Names: Jacobson, Bray, author.
Title: The Rocky Mountains / Bray Jacobson.
Description: New York : Gareth Stevens Publishing, 2023. | Series: Wonderful natural wonders | Includes index.
Identifiers: LCCN 2021036643 (print) | LCCN 2021036644 (ebook) | ISBN 9781538276907 (set) | ISBN 9781538276914 (library binding) | ISBN 9781538276891 (paperback) | ISBN 9781538276921 (ebook)
Subjects: LCSH: Rocky Mountains–Juvenile literature.
Classification: LCC F721 .J16 2023 (print) | LCC F721 (ebook) | DDC 978–dc23
LC record available at https://lccn.loc.gov/2021036643
LC ebook record available at https://lccn.loc.gov/2021036644

Published in 2023 by
Gareth Stevens Publishing
29 E. 21st Street
New York, NY 10010

Designer: Tanya Dellaccio
Editor: Kristen Nelson

Photo credits: Cover Tupungato/Shutterstock.com; background texture (pp 3-24) BEMPhoto_31/Shutterstock.com; p. 5 Andriy Blokhin/Shutterstock.com; p. 7 Rainer Lesniewski/Shutterstock.com; p. 9 Steven Castro/Shutterstock.com; p. 11 Lubomir Chudoba/Shutterstock.com; p. 13 Tampa/Shutterstock.com; p. 15 Pi-Lens/Shutterstock.com; p. 17 Gary L. Brewer/Shutterstock.com; p. 19 RosieRocket/Shutterstock.com; p. 21 NMS Photography/Shutterstock.com.

Printed in the United States of America

CPSIA compliance information: Batch #CSGS23: For further information contact Gareth Stevens, New York, New York at 1-800-542-2595.

CONTENTS

Boldface words appear in the glossary.

Into the Rockies

The largest mountain range in North America is certainly a natural wonder! The Rocky Mountains are also the second-longest mountain range in the world. They're more than 3,000 miles (4,800 km) long! In all, the mountains cover about 300,000 square miles (777,000 sq km).

The Long Range

The northernmost point of the Rocky Mountains is found in the U.S. state of Alaska. The range **extends** down through Canada into the United States all the way to New Mexico! The **Continental Divide** runs along the **crest** of the Rockies.

ALASKA
ROCKY MOUNTAINS
CANADA
MONTANA
IDAHO
WYOMING
UTAH
COLORADO
NEW MEXICO
UNITED STATES

The Rocky Mountains are part of a larger **system** of mountains. The Cordillera system includes the Rockies as well as the Sierra Navada, Cascade Range, and Coast Range. This system goes all the way to the tip of South America!

Lifting Up

The formation of the Rockies began millions of years ago. They formed through different periods of **uplift**. They were shaped by **erosion** and **glaciers** as well as rivers and streams moving though the land.

There are many **peaks** over 14,000 feet (4,267 m) in the Rocky Mountains. The highest is Mount Elbert. It's more than 14,430 feet (4,398 m) tall. Mount Elbert is in Colorado in a part of the Rockies called the Sawatch Range.

MOUNT ELBERT

River Start!

The longest river in North America, the Missouri River, starts in the Rocky Mountains. Other main rivers do too, including the Yellowstone, Platte, and Arkansas Rivers in the United States. In Canada, the Yukon River, among others, starts in the Rockies.

Climates Change

The Rocky Mountains stretch so far, there is a great range of **climates**. It's hot during New Mexico summers and very cold in Alaska and northern Canada, especially during winter. Wetter weather is more commonly found in the western parts of the mountains.

Many kinds of wildlife make their homes in the climates of the Rocky Mountains. Some of the best known are bighorn sheep, found throughout the range. Grizzly bears, antelopes, and caribou also live in the Rocky Mountains.

BIGHORN SHEEP

Protected Peaks

National and state parks in both the United States and Canada **protect** parts of the Rocky Mountains. Rocky Mountain National Park in Colorado was first established in 1915. In the park, there are more than 70 peaks taller than 12,000 feet (3,658 m)!

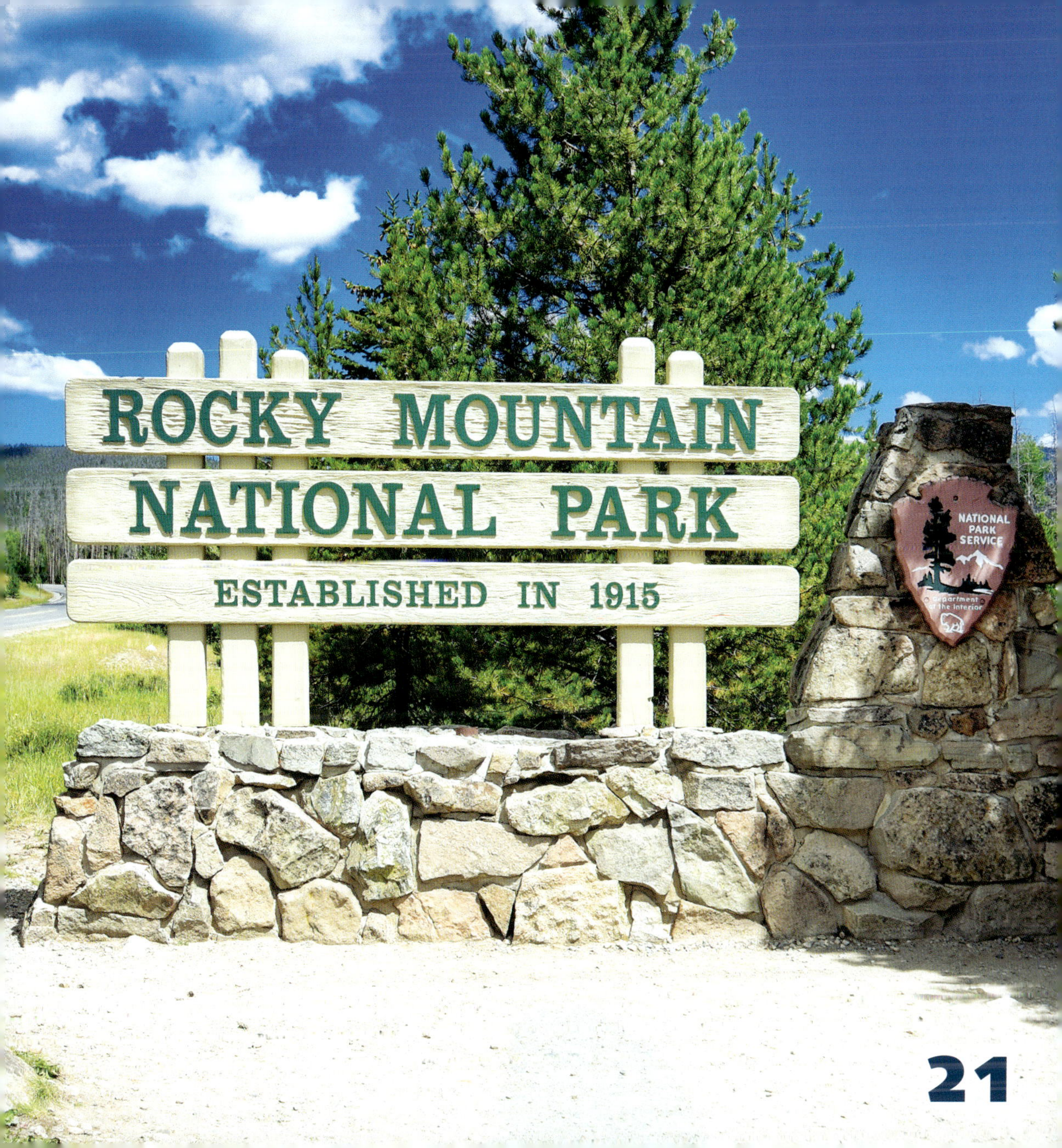
ROCKY MOUNTAIN
NATIONAL PARK
ESTABLISHED IN 1915
NATIONAL
PARK
SERVICE

GLOSSARY

climate: the average weather conditions of a place over a period of time

Continental Divide: the line of highest points of land separating the waters flowing west from those flowing north or east

crest: the highest point of something

erosion: the act of wearing away by water, wind, or ice

extend: to stretch out

glacier: a large area of ice that moves slowly down a slope or valley or over an area of land

peak: the pointed top of a mountain

protect: to keep safe

system: a group of similar parts that go together

uplift: the raising of Earth's surface because of natural processes

FOR MORE INFORMATION

BOOKS

Davies, Monika. *My Trip to the Rockies.* Huntington Beach, CA: Teacher Created Materials, 2021.

Josse, Barbara. *Lulu & Rocky in Rocky Mountain National Park.* Ann Arbor, MI: Sleeping Bear Press, 2021.

WEBSITES

Facts About the Rocky Mountains
www.dkfindout.com/us/earth/mountains/rocky-mountains/
Find out even more about this huge mountain range here.

Rocky Mountain National Park
www.nps.gov/romo/index.htm
Plan a trip to Rocky Mountain National Park and find out more about it on the National Park Service website.

Publisher's note to educators and parents: Our editors have carefully reviewed these websites to ensure that they are suitable for students. Many websites change frequently, however, and we cannot guarantee that a site's future contents will continue to meet our high standards of quality and educational value. Be advised that students should be closely supervised whenever they access the internet.

INDEX

leveled reader
social studies

WONDERFUL NATURAL WONDERS

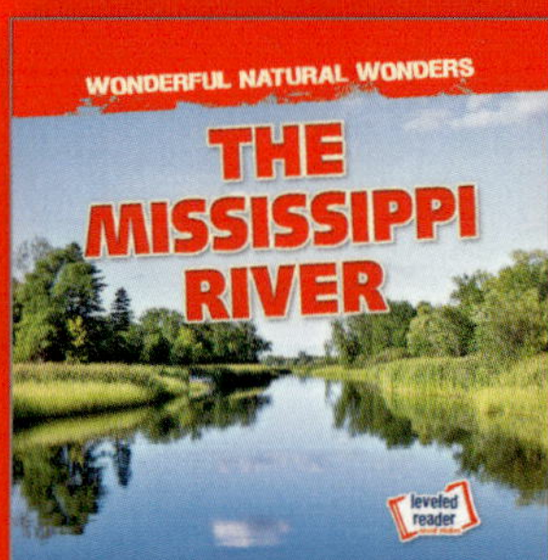

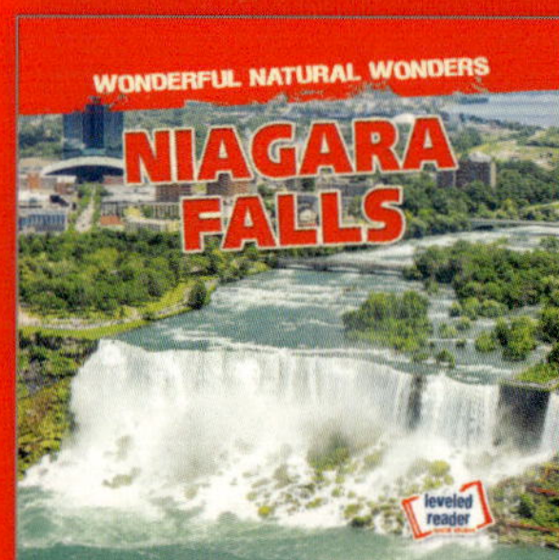

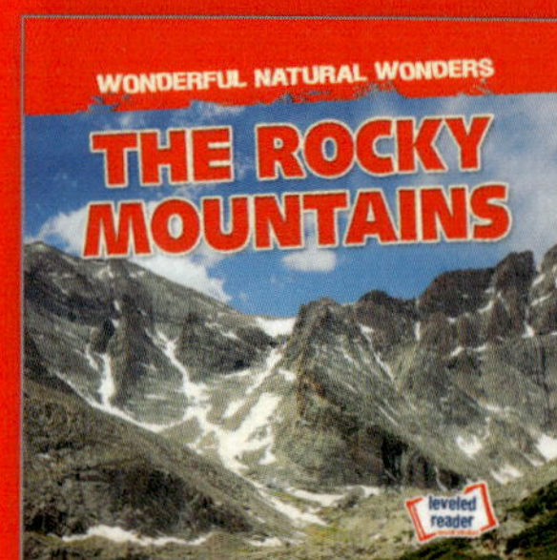

Gareth Stevens
PUBLISHING

ISBN: 9781538276891
6-pack ISBN: 9781538276907
9 781538 276891